Afghanistan

By Charles Piddock

Academic Consultant: Abraham Marcus
Associate Professor
Department of History and Center for Middle Eastern Studies
University of Texas at Austin

WORLD ALMANAC® LIBRARY

Please visit our Web site at: www.garethstevens.com
For a free color catalog describing World Almanac® Library's list of high-quality books
and multimedia programs, call 1-800-848-2928 (USA) or 1-800-387-3178 (Canada).
World Almanac® Library's fax: (414) 332-3567

Library of Congress Catalog-in-Publication Data

Piddock, Charles.
    Afghanistan / by Charles Piddock.
      p. cm. — (Nations in the news)
    Includes bibliographical references and index.
    ISBN-10: 0-8368-6706-8 — ISBN-13: 978-0-8368-6706-0 (lib. bdg.)
    ISBN-10: 0-8368-6713-0 — ISBN-13: 978-0-8368-6713-8 (softcover)
    1. Afghanistan—History—1989-2001—Juvenile literature.   2. Afghanistan—
  History—2001—Juvenile literature.   3. Afghanistan—History—Juvenile literature.
  I. Title.   II. Series: Piddock, Charles. Nations in the news.
  DS371.3.P53   2007
  958.104—dc22   2006011229

First published in 2007 by
World Almanac® Library
A Member of the WRC Media Family of Companies
330 West Olive Street, Suite 100
Milwaukee, WI 53212 USA

Copyright © 2007 by World Almanac® Library.

A Creative Media Applications, Inc. Production
Design and Production: Alan Barnett, Inc.
Editor: Susan Madoff
Copy Editor: Laurie Lieb
Proofreader: Laurie Lieb
Indexer: Nara Wood
World Almanac® Library editorial direction: Mark J. Sachner
World Almanac® Library editor: Gini Holland
World Almanac® Library art direction: Tammy West
World Almanac® Library production: Jessica Morris

Photo credits: Associated Press: cover and pages 5, 6, 7, 8, 10, 11, 12, 13, 14, 15, 16, 18, 19, 20, 21, 32, 34, 35, 36, 37, 38,
39, 40, 41, 42, 43; Northwind Pictures Archive: page 22; The Bridgeman Art Library:
pages 24, 26, 27; New York Public Library, Astor, Lenox and Tilden Foundations: page 25;
The Granger Collection: page 29; Maps courtesy of Ortelius Design

Printed in the United States of America

1 2 3 4 5 6 7 8 9 10 09 08 07 06

Table of Contents

Cover: An Afghan woman holds the election poster of Suraia Perlika, a candidate in the upcoming election, during her campaign in Kabul, Afghanistan, on September 14, 2005.

CHAPTER 1

Building a Nation

"This assembly is a sign of us regaining our honor," said Afghan president Hamid Karzai in a speech on December 19, 2005. Pausing to gain control of his emotions, he added, "This dear Afghanistan has risen again from the ashes.... We Afghans have the right to stand with honor and dignity with the international community."

Karzai was speaking before the 351 members of Afghanistan's newly

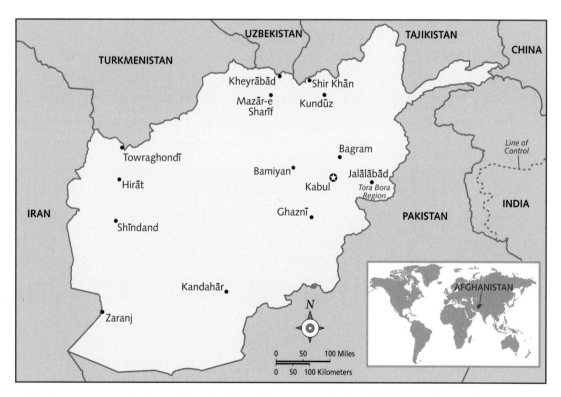

Afghanistan, a country in Central Asia of thirty million people, is bordered by Iran to the west, Turkmenistan, Uzbekistan, and Tajikistan in the north, Pakistan in the south and east, and China to the east.

On December 19, 2005, the first popularly elected parliament in Afghanistan in more than thirty years met at the inaugural session of the National Assembly in Kabul, the nation's capital. The meeting marked a major step toward democracy following the suppression of Taliban rule earlier in the year.

elected **parliament**. His emotion-filled words found an accepting audience. Everyone knew that only a few years before, in 2001, Afghanistan had been in the grip of a religious **dictatorship**. Under the rule of the **Taliban** (TAHL-e-bahn), music, movies, television, and Western clothing were banned. Men had to wear beards and women could not appear in public without having their entire bodies, including their faces, covered. Women were forbidden to work, and girls were not allowed to go to school.

Taliban rule began to crumble after the U.S.-led invasion on October 7, 2001, which began in response to the Taliban's refusal to turn over Osama bin Laden, the architect of the September 11, 2001, terror attacks on the United States. The invasion was followed by a war that lasted for two months. Anti-Taliban rebel forces, aided mainly by U.S. air power, overthrew the Taliban and chased **al-Qaeda** (al-KAY-duh), the terrorist organization led by bin Laden, from its bases in Afghanistan.

Today, Afghanistan has a new **constitution** guaranteeing freedoms, an elected president, and a democratically elected parliament. In the new

Afghanistan's president, Hamid Karzai (*shown left*), was born on December 24, 1957, in Kandahar, Afghanistan. He went to high school in Kabul and to college in Simla, India. In 1982, Karzai joined the fight against the Soviets, who had invaded Afghanistan in 1979. He rose to a high position in the Afghan **National Liberation Front**.

When the Taliban grew strong in the early 1990s, Karzai supported them. By 1994, however, he had turned against them because of their extreme interpretation of rule according to the laws of **Islam**. When they called for his death, he fled to safety in Pakistan. From Pakistan, Karzai worked to overthrow the Taliban. His efforts became a personal mission in 1999 when his father, Abdul Ahmad, was murdered by Taliban supporters on his way home from evening prayer. Karzai began to travel the world to rally support against Taliban rule.

In October 2001, shortly after the U.S.-led invasion, Karzai slipped back into Afghanistan. He worked with Afghan forces who were fighting the Taliban. Hearing that he was back in the country, the Taliban raided his hideout and searched for him. He was rescued by U.S. Special Forces only moments from capture.

On June 19, 2002, a special Afghan assembly appointed Karzai the country's interim president. On September 5, an assassin's bullet missed him by inches. On September 16, 2004, another attempt was made on Karzai's life when someone fired a rocket at the helicopter the president was riding in.

Hamid Karzai realized his life's goal when he was elected Afghanistan's president on October 9, 2004. He received 55.4 percent of the vote in the first democratic presidential election in the country's long history. When people question whether Karzai can overcome the **insurgents**, the **warlords**, and the drug trade, he answers confidently: "We will get it done.... Afghanistan has no option but to fight private military forces...corruption...[and] drugs. Without a major fight on these three fronts, Afghanistan will not see permanent stability."

parliament, 27.3 percent of the seats are reserved for women, giving them a strong voice in Afghanistan's government for the first time.

The Continuing War

Not all Afghans, however, support the new government. The Taliban and al-Qaeda are still fighting in eastern Afghanistan. The goal of these insurgents is to topple the government. "The parliament has been made up by invader Americans," said Taliban spokesman Qari Muhammad Yousuf Ahmadi. "We'll attack them as we attack the government and invading American **infidels**."

The stakes of the continuing war in Afghanistan are high. If Afghanistan's government falls, the forces of repression and terror will gain an important victory. Top U.S. officials, such as Secretary of State Condoleezza Rice and Vice President Dick Cheney, have recently visited Afghanistan to pledge U.S. support for the new government. Cheney was in the audience on December 19, 2005, to hear President Karzai's speech welcoming the new parliament.

Despite popular elections, Afghan insurgents continue to undermine the nation's commitment to democracy. In this January 2006 photo, soldiers of the International Security Assistance Force (the U.S.-led coalition) patrol the outskirts of Kabul, on the lookout for rebel groups planning to attack.

Some twenty thousand troops, mainly from the United States and the North Atlantic Treaty Organization (**NATO**), are trying to finish the job of wiping out the Taliban and al-Qaeda. It has proved very difficult to do, however, and in recent months the Taliban have actually stepped up their attacks.

Battling Poverty

President Karzai's government must not only battle the insurgent forces, but also solve the other major problems afflicting Afghanistan—poverty, powerful warlords, and a growing drug trade. Any one of these could threaten the survival of Afghan democracy.

Outside Kabul, Afghanistan's capital, and a few other cities, most Afghans practice a way of life little changed in a thousand years. Many remote areas have no electricity, running water, paved roads, hospitals, or schools. In 2004, Afghanistan was the seventh poorest country in the

Before the popular election of then interim president Hamid Karzai in 2004, seventeen candidates prepared to challenge his bid for the presidency in the historic vote. This picture shows candidate Abdul Hafiz Mansoor (right) listening to local residents during his unsuccessful campaign.

world, with life expectancy of about 44.5 years, according to the National Human Development Report. One out of five Afghan children dies before the age of five, and only 30 percent of all Afghans over the age of fifteen can read and write. Only 13 percent of Afghans have access to safe water, 12 percent to adequate sanitation, and 6 percent to electricity, according to the World Bank.

Billions of dollars of aid from the United States and the rest of the world flow into Afghanistan each year to construct highways, build schools and hospitals, and train doctors. The United States and other countries believe that if the Afghan government can give its people a better way of life, they will support the government and turn against those who would destroy it.

Taming the Warlords

According to Afghanistan's new constitution, the central government controls the country. In reality, though, the government's authority extends not much farther than the city limits of Kabul. Much of the rest of the country is effectively under the control of twelve powerful warlords. Some of the warlords command armies of ten thousand soldiers.

Powerful warlords are not new in Afghanistan. In fact, because the country has rarely had a strong central government, warlords have ruled for centuries. One reason is Afghanistan's rugged geography, which tends to isolate regions. Another reason is the sharp division between the country's different **ethnic** groups, whose loyalties are to families, tribes, and clans before country. If asked to describe themselves, Afghans will name their ethnic and tribal allegiance rather than calling themselves Afghans.

The two major ethnic groups in Afghanistan today are the **Pashtuns** and **Tajiks**. President Karzai belongs to the Pashtuns, who have controlled much of Afghanistan for centuries. The Pashtuns are further divided into smaller groups with fierce local loyalties and traditions. Loyalty to one's tribal or clan leader and the clan's code always comes first. That is how the warlords maintain their power. **Pukhtunwali**, the Pashtun code, for example, has a much stronger role in a Pashtun's life than any possible law passed by parliament. At the core of Pukhtunwali is a sense of family and tribal honor. Any insult to the family or village must be avenged.

One of President Karzai's goals is to gradually replace codes such as Pukhtunwali with a sense of national loyalty among Afghans. To accomplish this goal, he must lessen the power of the warlords. Right now,

Osama bin Laden (*shown left*) was born in 1957 into a wealthy family in Saudi Arabia. His father, Muhammad Awad bin Laden, was the owner of the largest construction company in the country.

The family was very religious, and Osama bin Laden was a devout Muslim. When the Soviet Union invaded Afghanistan in 1979, he was outraged that the "godless" Soviets had attacked a Muslim nation. (The Soviet Union was a communist nation with an official policy of **atheism**.) Bin Laden went to Afghanistan to join other Muslims in fighting the Soviets. In 1986, he set up his own guerrilla training camps for fighters from Arab Muslim countries. At that time, the United States, still engaged in a Cold War with the Soviets, became the chief provider of weapons and aid to the anti-Soviet rebels, including foreign fighters such as bin Laden. Two years later, in 1988, bin Laden founded **al-Qaeda** to keep track of the Arab fighters and aid their fight.

After the Soviets withdrew, bin Laden returned to Saudi Arabia. In 1990, he was shocked and angered when the Saudi government invited U.S. troops to be stationed in Saudi Arabia in order to prepare to fight Iraqi dictator Saddam Hussein, who had invaded Kuwait. Bin Laden thought it wrong to station unbelievers in Islam's holiest land. He recruited several thousand men to wage war against the American military force and sent them to training camps in Afghanistan. In 1998, he sent out a message to Muslims everywhere, saying "To kill the Americans and their allies—civilian and military—is an individual duty for every Muslim who can do it in any country in which it is possible to do it."

Before al-Qaeda's attacks on the United States on September 11, 2001, bin Laden orchestrated several other attacks on U.S. targets. In 1993, al-Qaeda terrorists set off a truck bomb in the basement garage of New York's World Trade Center. In 1996, al-Qaeda bombed U.S. barracks in Saudi Arabia, killing nineteen Americans. In October 2000, al-Qaeda agents bombed the destroyer USS *Cole* in the port of Aden.

Bin Laden today is thought to be in hiding somewhere in Afghanistan or Pakistan. In January 2006, in the first video message sent by him in over a year, he threatened to attack the United States again. Bin Laden offered to accept a truce if the United States withdrew its forces from Iraq and Afghanistan.

Karzai has kept the warlords' loyalty by appointing a number of them to important government positions. Meanwhile, he is building up a national Afghan army that will be larger than any warlord's army.

Fighting the Insurgents

The leader of the Taliban is **Mullah** Muhammad Omar. Mullah Omar and Osama bin Laden, along with other top Taliban and al-Qaeda leaders, are still directing the insurgency against Karzai. Both men are suspected to be hiding somewhere in the rugged mountains that line the border between Afghanistan and Pakistan. Mullah Omar and bin Laden have been joined by another insurgent group called Hezb-e Islami. Its leader, Gulbuddin Hekmatyar, has declared a **jihad** against Karzai and Western troops in Afghanistan. U.S. experts estimate that there are about two thousand active Taliban fighters and several hundred fighters linked to Hezb-e Islami. No one is sure of the number of al-Qaeda fighters.

The insurgents have killed Western aid workers and kidnapped other foreigners. They have tried to assassinate President Karzai and have killed many of Karzai's top officials. They now conduct daily attacks in Afghanistan. By mid-October 2005, thirteen hundred fighters, most of them insur-

Gulbuddin Hekmatyar, an Afghan warlord and leader of the Afghanistan Islamic Party, was instrumental in ending the Soviet occupation of Afghanistan. He served as prime minister twice in the 1990s and now opposes Hamid Karzai's government and the presence of U.S. troops in Afghanistan. Currently in hiding due to his ties to Osama bin Laden, he is reportedly living in Jabal Saraj, east of Kabul, Afghanistan.

gents, had been killed since the Karzai government took over. At least eighty-four Americans died in Afghanistan in 2005, more than in any other year since the United States invaded in 2001. The violence and deaths continue in 2006.

Afghan farmers pick opium in Kandahar in April 2005. The United Nations Office on Drugs and Crime reported in March 2006 that Afghan farmers are planting more opium poppies than last year, despite a U.S.-sponsored crackdown on the world's largest illegal narcotics industry.

Tackling the Drug Trade

The danger to the Afghan government from the insurgents, however, may already be dwarfed by another threat: the illegal drug trade.

Afghanistan today produces more than 80 percent of the world's supply of opium. Opium is obtained from poppies grown by farmers in Afghanistan's remote mountain valleys. The drug is then smuggled out of the country and processed into heroin. The heroin makes its way into Europe and North America, where it is sold to drug addicts. Together, farmers, warlords, and corrupt Afghan officials make money through the trade. Experts say that this drug trade now provides a startling 50 percent of the money in Afghanistan's economy. The drug trade is so powerful in Afghanistan's economy that the U.S. State Department declared in 2003 that the country was "on the verge of becoming a narcotics state." A "narcotics state" is a country where political or economic power is significantly involved in the manufacture and sale of illegal drugs.

Several months before the U.S. invasion, the Taliban brutally cut back on poppy farming, imprisoning and beating anyone caught processing or selling opium. When the Taliban were ousted, however, the drug trade began to recover rapidly. It generated an estimated $2.3 billion in 2003, much of it going into the pockets of the warlords and their supporters. The drug business has also reached far into the national government. In late September 2005, Ali Jalili, Afghanistan's interior minister, resigned. He had complained for months that top officials in the government were helping drug traffickers and felt that nothing would be done to stop it.

Cutting Off Drug Money

Money from the opium trade is also funding the insurgents. Mirwais Yasini, head of Afghanistan's Counter Narcotics Directorate, estimates that al-Qaeda, the Taliban, and Hezb-e Islami receive more than $150 million a year from drug sales. One report says that al-Qaeda agents in Pakistan received 4,000 pounds (1,816 kilograms) of heroin to sell every other month in 2005.

In February 2005, President Karzai called a two-day meeting of tribal elders and officials to look for ways to get Afghanistan's 2.3 million farmers to give up poppy farming. Everyone agreed that some way must be found to get farmers to raise crops that will

earn them the same amount of money that poppy farming gives them. Afghan officials also say that the government must put drug dealers in prison and clean up the corruption that reaches to the highest levels of the government. "If we fail [to stem the drug trade], we will fail as a country and eventually we will fall back into the hands of terrorism," Karzai said. That, of course, would be a major defeat for both democracy and for the war on terror.

An Afghan counter-narcotics soldier uses a scale to weigh bags of opium that were found hidden in the hull of a fuel tanker in Kabul on May 26, 2005. President Hamid Karzai has come under fire for his record in fighting the drug trade.

CHAPTER 2

Afghanistan's Neighbors

fghanistan's future does not depend just on Afghanistan. It also depends on what happens in the two major countries that border it—Pakistan and Iran. Pakistan has nearly eight times the population of Afghanistan. Iran has four times Afghanistan's population and twelve times the land area.

A Relatively New Nation

Pakistan is a relatively new nation. It came into existence on August 14, 1947, when the British colony of India

Pakistani prime minister Shaukat Aziz (left) meets with Afghan president Hamid Karzai at a conference at the Presidential Palace in Kabul in July 2005. Despite Aziz's pledge to fight terrorism and extremism alongside Afghanistan, violence continues to flare in both countries.

Kuchi nomads (shown above) *are Pashtuns who migrate with their flocks from southern Afghanistan and Pakistan, where they spend the winter, to pasturelands in the mountains of central Afghanistan in the summer.*

was partitioned, or broken apart into two nations, by agreement between Great Britain and Indian **Hindu** and Muslim leaders. One of the nations was India, with a mainly Hindu population. The other was Pakistan, with a mostly Muslim population. Pakistan was created with two parts: West Pakistan, which bordered Iran, Afghanistan, and India, and East Pakistan, which bordered India and Burma (now Myanmar). East Pakistan

and West Pakistan were separated by 1,000 miles (1,600 kilometers) of Indian territory. In 1971, East Pakistan broke away to become Bangladesh. Today's Pakistan is the former West Pakistan.

The people who today live in Pakistan's Northwest Border Province have long been closely related to the people of Afghanistan. They are Pashtuns—relatives of the Pashtuns who make up 44 percent of

The United States' steadfast friend in the region is Pakistan's president, Pervez Musharraf (*shown left*). Musharraf, a devout Muslim, is an army general who took control of Pakistan in 1999 with a group of other generals. He formally declared himself president on June 20, 2001. On January 1, 2004, in a formal vote of confidence, Musharraf won more than half the votes in the electoral college of Pakistan. Thus, according to Pakistan's constitution, he was "deemed to be elected" to the office of the president until national elections in October 2007.

Musharraf supports the war on terror with more than words. He has sent Pakistani army troops into combat against the insurgents who cross the border into Pakistan. He regularly aids U.S. forces in their search for bin Laden. While his support earns him praise from U.S. president George W. Bush, it has gotten him in some trouble at home. In the four years he has led Pakistan, there have been several attempts on his life. On December 14, 2003, a powerful bomb went off only minutes after his motorcade crossed a bridge. Nine days later, on December 25, two suicide bombers tried to kill Musharraf, but their bombs failed to kill the president. Sixteen other people were killed instead.

Afghanistan's population. This close connection exists because modern national boundaries have cut through age-old tribal and ethnic areas. Religious or political movements among the Pashtuns that begin on one side of the Afghan-Pakistani border quickly spread to the other side. Between 1979 and 1989, many thousands of Pakistanis crossed the border to help the Afghans fight the Soviets. Pakistan's government, along with the United States, aided the rebels with weapons and money.

Pakistan also supported the Taliban. Pakistani leaders felt that the Taliban would end the civil war in Afghanistan that followed the Soviet withdrawal. Many of the Taliban fighters were Pashtuns who had studied in **madrasas** in Pakistan.

After the terrorist attacks of September 11, 2001, on New York City and Washington, D.C., the

Taliban refused to turn over Osama bin Laden to Pakistan, which quickly withdrew its support. Pakistani president Pervez Musharaf threw his support behind the United States and Afghan president Hamid Karzai. Today, Pakistani troops help the U.S. and Afghan effort to fight the insurgency in Afghanistan.

Trade and Aid

Trade between nations usually strengthens friendly ties. Pakistan buys wool, cotton, and other goods from Afghanistan. Pakistan sends manufactured goods and other products to Afghanistan. In 2002, the trade between the two countries amounted to only about $20 million. By 2004, however, the value of Afghan-Pakistani trade had soared to over $1 billion.

Other ties between the two countries also grew. In 2004, Pakistan pledged over $100 million in aid to Afghanistan. In July 2005, Pakistan's prime minister, Shaukat Aziz, and President Karzai agreed to begin construction of a new railroad line between the two countries. They also agreed to increase the number of airline flights between Afghanistan and Pakistan and to step up cooperation in the war against terrorists.

"Afghanistan and Pakistan are like twins…joined in the body," said President Karzai during a visit to Pakistan. "If one of them gets hurt, it will definitely hurt the other. When terrorism affects Afghanistan, it also affects Pakistan. We have suffered in the past at the hands of terrorists, attacking our **mosques**, our schools, our clergy, our candidates for elections and our women and children. The same has happened in Pakistan."

Problems Still Remain

Despite the growing cooperation between Pakistan and Afghanistan, significant problems remain. One centers on the large number of Afghan refugees living in Pakistan. Most of them fled to Pakistan during the years following the Soviet invasion. Now they live in camps in the Northwest Frontier Province and are a drain on Pakistan's resources. In 2005, the United Nations Refugee Agency helped more than 400,000 refugees to

FAST FACT

The proposal to carve a Muslim nation from British India was first made in 1930 by the Indian Muslim poet Muhammad Iqbal. Iqbal suggested that the four northwestern provinces of India be joined in such a nation. In a 1933 pamphlet, a university student named Choudhary Rahmat Ali invented the name *Pakistan* for the proposed nation. The name is derived from the Urdu words *Pak* (meaning "pure") and *stan* (meaning "country").

Pakistani police officers look at a burned-out bus that was set on fire by an angry mob of protesters in April 2005. The riots began when the MMA called for a general strike that shut down parts of Pakistan.

return to Afghanistan, but a count of the refugees by the Pakistani government in March 2005 showed that there were still more than three million refugees in Pakistan. Pakistan would like Afghanistan to encourage the refugees to return.

Another worry for Pakistan is the growth in support for the Taliban and al-Qaeda among the Pashtun population. In Peshawar, capital of the Northwest Frontier Province, many people consider Mullah Omar and Osama bin Laden heroes. In addition, support for an Islamic political party that admires the Taliban has mushroomed. The Muttahida Majlis-e-Amal (MMA) party now controls 20 percent of Pakistan's parliament. The MMA wants to establish a stricter observance of Islamic principles in Pakistan. The MMA opposes

President Musharraf for his opposition to the Taliban and for his support of the United States.

Iran and Afghanistan

Afghanistan also has deep cultural and historical ties with Iran. Like Pakistan, Iran has played a major role in Afghanistan's history. Many times in the past, the rulers of Iran controlled large parts of Afghanistan, leaving the mark of Persian culture. The Tajiks, who make up about one-quarter of Afghanistan's population, are descended from Iranians and speak a language similar to Persian, the language of Iran.

Iran, unlike Pakistan, never supported the Taliban. The Iranians did not want the Taliban's form of Islam to spread to Iran. Iranian leaders were glad to see the Taliban defeated and pushed out of power, even though it was Iran's sworn enemy, the United States, which achieved that success.

Afghan refugees line up to board a vehicle that will take them from their camp in Peshawar, Pakistan, back to Afghanistan on August 30, 2005. Almost three million refugees have returned to Afghanistan since 2002. More than three million still remain in refugee camps in Pakistan and Iran.

An Afghan woman walks next to a building in Herat, near the border of Afghanistan and Iran. The writing on the building reads "Death to Katami, Long Live Ahmedinejad," referring to Iran's new president, Mahmoud Ahmedinejad, who replaced Muhammad Katami in the June 2006 elections. Afghan officials fear that the hard-line Islamic regime of Iran's new president will have a negative influence on Afghanistan.

Iran and the United States have been hostile to each other since the 1979 revolution that deposed the shah, or king, of Iran. The United States had supported the shah. Beginning in November 1979, Iranian **revolutionaries** held American hostages for 444 days before releasing them. The United States broke off relations with Iran and today the two nations do not officially recognize each other.

In spite of the hostility between them, both Iran and the United States support Afghanistan's present government. At a conference to write a new Afghan constitution, held in Bonn, Germany, in December 2001, for example, Iran played a major role in getting various Afghan groups to work together. At the same time, Iran pledged $560 million in aid to help Afghanistan rebuild from years of war.

Roads and Refugees

Iran has consistently strengthened economic and trade cooperation with Afghanistan. Iranian businesses view Afghanistan as potentially a huge market for Iranian products. Iran also hopes that it can help Afghan farmers replace poppy cultivation with other crops, thus ridding the entire region of the drug trade. A large part of the trade goes through Iran to **Persian Gulf** ports. The drug trade, by increasing lawlessness and corruption in both nations, hurts Iran as well as Afghanistan. Drug abuse has exploded in Iran in recent years.

In January 2005, President Karzai traveled to Iran to celebrate the official opening of a new road linking the Doqarum border region of northeastern Iran with the Afghan city of Herat. Iran had recently completed work on the road, which both countries hope will boost trade. Iran is also building a road from its Persian Gulf port of Bandar-e Abbas up through landlocked Afghanistan. When completed, this road is expected to provide a quick, efficient way to transport goods from the Persian Gulf to the interior of Afghanistan.

Iran, like Pakistan, has become home to a large number of Afghan refugees. More than two million fled to Iran to escape the fighting. More than 800,000 still live in Iran. Iran wants them to return home.

Afghan girls, photographed in July 2004, study at a special school designed to prepare them to return to regular classes. An estimated 4.5 million children in Afghanistan, two-thirds of them girls, received little or no formal education during the five years of Taliban rule.

CHAPTER 3

A Turbulent History

The history of Afghanistan has been heavily influenced by its geographical position. For thousands of years, it has been at the center of two great overland trade routes. One route went east and west, from China to the Middle East and Europe. The other went south and north, from India to central Asia. For many centuries, caravans traveled these routes, bringing goods through Afghanistan. Periodically, conquering armies traveled the trade routes, often bringing death and destruction to Afghanistan. Among Afghanistan's invaders have been Persians, Greeks, Arabs, Mongols, British, and Soviets.

Early History

What we know of Afghanistan's very early history comes from evidence found by archaeologists. It shows that Indo-Europeans, people similar to the ancient Iranians, were living as nomadic herders in Afghanistan as early as 6000 B.C. By 3000 B.C. the inhabitants were no longer nomads but lived in small villages, making pottery and trading with the Elamites, who lived in ancient Iran, and the ancient Egyptians. By 1500 B.C., the ancestors of the Pashtuns and Tajiks had started to populate Afghanistan.

A hand-colored woodcut shows caravans of traders traveling along the Silk Road in ancient Central Asia.

In 540 B.C. northern Afghanistan was conquered by the ancient Persians, whose homeland was present-day Iran under **Cyrus the Great**. Cyrus was the founder of the **Achaemenid Empire**, centered in modern Iran. The empire once controlled a vast area of land from present-day Turkey and Egypt to present-day India. By 500 B.C., Cyrus's son, Darius I, had extended the empire's boundaries to include all of present-day Afghanistan. The area was divided into several satrapies, or provinces, of the empire. The northwest satrapy was called Bactria. The Persians, like every other conqueror of Afghanistan, had trouble keeping order. It is recorded that Bactria and the other parts of Afghanistan required more than the usual number of Persian troops to keep the peace.

Greeks and Kushans

Persian rule of Afghanistan was followed by Greek rule. In 329 B.C., after conquering the other provinces of the Achaemenid Empire, Alexander the Great moved his armies into Afghanistan. He conquered it after a series of fierce battles.

When Alexander died in 323 B.C., his generals fought for power among themselves. Afghanistan fell into the hands of one of the generals, Seleucus, but not for long. In 304 B.C. Seleucus was defeated in battle by an Indian king named Chandragupta Maurya. Chandragupta took control of southern Afghanistan.

During the reigns of Chandragupta and his successors, a new religion took root in Afghanistan: **Buddhism**. Buddhism was founded in northern India in the fifth century B.C. by Gautama, known as "the enlightened one," or the Buddha. The Buddha taught that humans could attain enlightenment, or complete understanding, and end suffering. The Buddha died in 483 B.C. His followers, however, continued to grow in numbers. Today, Buddhism is one of the world's major religions, with followers on every continent. There are no practicing Buddhists, however, in Afghanistan at this time.

FAST FACT

In trade along the Silk Road, China received grapes, cotton, chestnuts, and pomegranates from the West in exchange for Chinese silk and other goods. Chinese methods for smelting iron, making paper, and other industrial techniques spread to the West along the road. The Romans often paid for Chinese goods with precious metals, particularly gold. By A.D. 10, China's gold reserves are thought to have been larger than Europe's. Some historians think that the imbalance may have seriously hurt the Roman economy over time, possibly contributing to the fall of Rome.

The steps, terraces, and temple dedicated to the Kushan emperor Kaniska can be seen among the ruins of this site located in Surkh-Kotal, Afghanistan.

Around A.D. 50, new tribes began migrating to Afghanistan from China. One of these tribes was the Kushans, who converted to Buddhism. The Kushans settled along the trade routes and grew rich from handling trade. They founded an empire along what became the Silk Road, which ran from China to the Roman Empire. The Kushans produced a number of magnificent statues and other pieces of Buddhist art. The greatest Kushan ruler was Kaniska, who ruled the empire between 78 and 103.

The Arab Invaders

In 652, yet another group of invaders arrived in Afghanistan. These newcomers were Arabs, and they brought another new religion: Islam. Islam was founded by the Prophet Muhammad (570–632) in what is now Saudi Arabia. The new religion quickly spread throughout the Arabian Peninsula, carried by Arab armies that won battle after battle. What is now Iraq and Iran were also conquered for Islam. The Arabs ruled Afghanistan for only two hundred years, but Islam quickly replaced Buddhism as Afghanistan's main religion.

In 962, Turkish rulers took over Afghanistan from local chieftains, founding the Ghaznavid dynasty. The most famous leader of this dynasty was Mahmud of Ghazna. He ruled from 998 to 1030. Mahmud was a brilliant military leader who extended the boundaries of his empire to include much of Iran and large parts of what is now Pakistan and India. He filled his capital city of Ghazna (now Ghazni in present-day Afghanistan) with new palaces, gardens, monuments, and mosques. Hundreds of artists, poets, and scholars flocked to his court. Among them was the famous Persian poet, Firdawsi.

The Mongols

Tragedy struck Afghanistan in the early 1200s, when the Mongol armies of Genghis Khan (1162–1227) swooped down on Afghanistan. The Mongols invaded because ambassadors they had

This painting shows the tomb of Mahmud of Ghazna, who claimed the throne of Afghanistan in 998.

sent to Afghanistan as part of a trading caravan were mistaken for spies. A local Afghan ruler had many of them killed and burned the beards of the others as an insult.

When Genghis Khan learned what had been done to his ambassadors, he flew into a rage and then marched to Afghanistan. The Mongols leveled the city of Herat and killed all its inhabitants, including its animals. They then destroyed the city of Balkh, dumping all the books from its famous library into the river. According to legend, the Mongols thus destroyed over one million beautiful volumes, "enough to choke the river."

Genghis Khan was not satisfied with just killing. His troops also poured salt over Afghanistan's farmland, making it unfit to grow crops. They destroyed Afghanistan's wells and irrigation canals by filling them with sand. For more than one hundred years, Afghanistan suffered Mongol rule. Then the Mongols' power weakened and local chieftains were able to take control once again.

Another Mongol invasion of Afghanistan took place under Tamerlane (1336–1405), who had conquered a great empire in the late 1370s. This time, however, Tamerlane rebuilt what his ancestors had destroyed. He rebuilt Herat as his capital and filled it with beautiful build-

ings. Tamerlane's descendants ruled for a hundred years before Afghanistan fell apart again under local rulers. As before, it was reunited once again, this time under Babur (1483–1530). Babur conquered eastern Afghanistan and made Kabul his capital. He loved the city, finding its climate and scenery delightful. When Babur died, he was

Genghis Khan, the Mongol king, conquered Afghanistan in the early 1200s.

Tamerlane the Great

Tamerlane's real name was Timur. The Europeans called him Tamerlane after the Persian name Timur-i Lang, or "Timur the Lame," because he walked with a limp from an old arrow wound. In his time, he was known as Tamerlane the Great because he conquered a greater empire than even Alexander the Great had. Tamerlane's armies were victorious from India to the outskirts of Moscow.

Tamerlane was born near the central Asian city of Samarkand in 1336. He was the son of a local chieftain who claimed descent from Genghis Khan. Tamerlane was famous for his intelligence. Although he never learned to read and write, he spoke three languages and liked to hear about history while he ate his meals. He loved and appreciated art and architecture and was said to be a master chess player.

Tamerlane died while preparing to take a 200,000-man army to conquer China. The great conqueror is fondly remembered in Afghanistan, where he rebuilt Herat and other cities.

buried in a garden in Kabul that he had planted himself. Afghans still make pilgrimages to his tomb.

The centuries after Babur's death were centuries of disunity. In the sixteenth century, India and Iran held between them the territory of Afghanistan. Beginning in 1747, however, Ahmad Khan Durrani, the Afghan commander of the Iranian shah's bodyguard, took control in Afghanistan, which, for the first time, emerged as a separate country. He proved to be a great king who reformed Afghanistan's criminal law and encouraged painting, poetry, and architecture. Today Afghans regard him as the "Father of the Nation."

Russia and Britain

In the 1700s and 1800s, two European powers, Russia and Great

Ahmad Khan Abdali

In October 1747, Ahmad Khan Abdali was proclaimed shah, or king, of Afghanistan by an assembly of Pashtun chiefs. He took the name Durr-i Duran, which means "pearl of pearls" and became known as Ahmad Shah Durrani. The Pashtun tribesmen rallied to the new king's banner. He led them to a number of conquests that greatly expanded the kingdom of Afghanistan, adding much of present-day Pakistan and large parts of India and eastern Iran.

Durrani is honored in Afghanistan today much as George Washington is honored in the United States. The king was an outstanding general and a just ruler. He governed with the help of a council of tribal chiefs and had the overwhelming loyalty of the Afghan people. When the king died in 1773, he left twenty-three sons. Several of them ruled after him.

Britain, became involved in Afghanistan. Britain was expanding its territories in India and had its eye on northern India (now Pakistan) near Afghanistan. By the early 1700s, Russia had started expanding its empire southward, looking for warm weather ports (outlets to the sea that did not freeze over in winter). Russian rulers needed such ports to expand Russia's trade. So, while Britain was expanding northward in India, Russia was expanding southward in central Asia. The two nations were about to clash—in Afghanistan.

When Dost Muhammad Khan, who ruled Afghanistan from 1826, declared war on a local ruler in northern India, he asked for British help. The British refused, because they did not trust the Afghans. Besides, they wanted northern India for themselves. Turned down by the British, Dost Muhammad asked the Russians for help. Alarmed, the British sent an army into Afghanistan to punish Dost Muhammad.

This first Anglo-Afghan War lasted from 1839 to 1842. The British quickly captured Ghazna, Kandahar, and Kabul. They deposed Dost Muhammad and put a former ruler, Shah Shuja, on the throne. The Afghans hated Shah Shuja and revolted. Afghan fighters launched attack after attack against the British army in Kabul, forcing the British to retreat toward India. More than 4,000 British and Indian soldiers and 12,500 camp followers tried to leave

Afghanistan through the mountains. Almost all were killed by Afghans or perished in the ice and snow before they reached Jalalabad at the Khyber Pass, the gateway to India.

The second Anglo-Afghan War lasted from 1878 to 1880. It began when the Afghan ruler, Sher Ali Khan, welcomed a Russian diplomatic mission to Kabul and refused a British mission. Furious at the insult, the British launched an invasion and drove Sher Ali from the throne. They replaced him with his nephew Abdal-Rahman Khan. During his reign, which lasted from 1880 to 1901, Abdur Rahman established a strong national army, crushed tribal warlords, abolished slavery, and set up a national system of courts. It was during this time that the Russians and British established the permanent borders that Afghanistan has today.

In the 1930s, another Afghan king, Muhammad Zahir Shah, tried to modernize the country. He founded the University of Kabul, built new highways, and set up a national bank.

A contemporary engraving shows the British army camped outside Kabul during the first Anglo-Afghan War.

In 1973, Muhammad Daoud Khan, who had been the king's prime minister, overthrew Muhammad Zahir and declared Afghanistan a republic. In 1978, Zahir was overthrown by the pro-Soviet commanders of Afghanistan's army.

Soviet Invasion

The army commanders moved quickly to establish communism and to gain the support of the Afghan people. They called for land reform. They proposed free education for all. At the same time, they killed and imprisoned those who disagreed with them, especially Islamic leaders. Thousands of Soviet advisers arrived to help run the government. The great portion of Afghanistan's population was devoutly Muslim and strongly opposed to communism and Soviet control because of Soviet atheism. To Afghan Muslims, Soviet control posed a great threat to their religious beliefs.

The result was a series of revolts across the country. Warlords declared their independence. Muslim leaders called for a holy war. In the face of this mounting opposition, the Afghan government leaders called for Soviet troops to help. On December 26, 1979, battle tanks from the Soviet Union rumbled across the Soviet-Afghan border.

The large and well-equipped Soviet military expected a quick victory over the Afghan rebels, who called them-

The Cold War

The struggle in Afghanistan between the mujahideen and the Soviets was part of a much larger world struggle called the Cold War (1945–1990). The Cold War was a battle for political and economic dominance between a group of communist nations, led by the Soviet Union, and a group of Western nations, led by the United States. It is called the Cold War because it never developed into an actual fighting "hot war" between the United States and the Soviet Union. Nevertheless, both nations engaged in a nuclear arms race and sponsored small, nonnuclear conflicts around the world. The Korean War (1950–1953) and the Vietnam War (1964–1975) were two such conflicts. U.S. support for the mujahideen in Afghanistan was motivated mainly by U.S. desire to inflict a defeat on the Soviet Union as part of the Cold War. Similarly, U.S. president Jimmy Carter ordered a U.S. boycott of the 1980 Olympic Games in Moscow to protest the Soviet invasion of Afghanistan. In 1991 the huge Soviet Union collapsed into fifteen separate countries, including Russia.

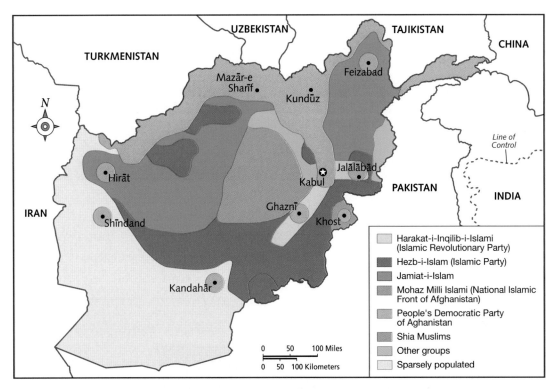

This 1987 map shows the different fighting forces in Afghanistan during the Soviet occupation. The ten-year war between Soviet troops and anti-government rebel groups — of varying ethnicities and political ideologies fighting to depose the Soviet-based government — destroyed the mountainous nation and fractured the population.

selves **mujahideen**, or "holy warriors." That didn't happen. The mujahideen had the support of the countryside. They were also well armed and organized with the help of the United States and Pakistan. The Soviets poured money, weapons, and soldiers into Afghanistan, but after almost ten years, they controlled only Kabul and a few other cities. The mujahideen controlled the rest of the country. By 1989, more than fifty thousand Soviet soldiers had been killed or wounded, and the Soviets, realizing they could not win the war, withdrew. Afghanistan's communist government gradually collapsed as a result of this war and many other causes, and the mujahideen now were in charge of a ruined country. Like the Mongols in the 1200s, the Soviets had destroyed forests, clogged up irrigation canals, burned crops, and killed farm animals. Between five and six million Afghans had fled to safety in Pakistan and Iran. More than one and one-half million Afghans had died in the conflict.

CHAPTER 4

The Rise
of the Taliban

The Soviet withdrawal left Afghanistan still at war. Afghanistan's communist government controlled Kabul. The mujahideen controlled the countryside.

The two sides continued to fight for three more years until April 1992, when the mujahideen captured Kabul and the government fell. Still, the war-weary country found no rest.

Osama bin Laden (center) is joined by Egyptian Islamic militants Ayman al-Zawahiri (left) and Muhammad Atef (right) at a 1989 meeting in Afghanistan. Atef, who officials believe helped plan the September 11, 2001, terrorist attacks in New York City, was allegedly killed by U.S. air strikes on Kabul in November 2001. The banner behind the three men quotes a verse from the Koran, Islam's holy book.

Mullah Omar

Mullah Omar, the leader of the Taliban, was born in either 1959 or 1961 in a small Afghan village. The son of a peasant farmer, he grew up very poor, living in a mud hut. After studying at a madrasa, he became the local mullah, or Islamic religious leader, in the village of Sangesar. He lost his right eye fighting with the mujahideen, earning him the nickname of *rund*, or "one-eyed."

Mullah Omar experiences dreams in which, he says, God tells him what to do. In 1994, he had a dream that Allah came to him in the shape of a man. Allah asked him to lead the faithful and establish a Muslim nation that would practice a very strict interpretation of the Koran. God's goal for him in the dream was to "cleanse" Afghan society and reestablish the true rule of the Koran.

Omar, although shy and a poor public speaker, was inspired to start a movement. Thousands of fighters—Afghans, Pakistanis, and other Muslims—joined him to form the Taliban. In 1996, Mullah Omar accepted the title of "commander of the faithful" offered by his followers and wrapped himself in a cloak said to have belonged to the Prophet Muhammad himself.

In 2001, a Pakistani official went to Mullah Omar to try to save the Bamiyan Buddha statues. Omar described to him another dream he had had about "a mountain falling down on him." Before it hit, Omar said, God appeared and asked why Omar did nothing to get rid of the false idols. He therefore allowed the Taliban to destroy the statues.

There is only one known photograph of Mullah Omar. Taken before his injury, it shows a black-bearded, turbaned man with piercing eyes.

The mujahideen began fighting among themselves. Each of the groups that composed the mujahideen had its own vision of Afghanistan's future. Each also wanted to run the country. So they fought with each other for control.

In 1994, a new force entered the fight. This was the Taliban. The word *Taliban* means "religious students." Many members of the Taliban had been students at madrasas, in Pakistan.

At the time the Soviets withdrew, Mullah Omar, the eventual leader of the Taliban, was running a small madrasa near Kandahar. Villagers complained to Omar about attacks from local thugs. Omar responded by giving rifles to his students and enforcing order, often by capturing suspected criminals and executing them.

Success led to success, and volunteers flocked to the banner of

An unidentified man is covered in garbage and paraded through the streets of Kabul after being convicted of stealing 2.6 gallons (10 liters) of gasoline in February 1997. The Taliban's strict law says that the punishment for thievery is to chop off a convict's hands. Those convicted of minor theft (like this man), however, are punished with public humiliation.

the Taliban. Saudi Arabia and Pakistan supplied the Taliban with money and volunteers. By 1998, the Taliban had gained control of nearly 90 percent of Afghanistan. Many Afghans welcomed the Taliban because they finally brought peace by ending the fighting that had plagued the country for so many years.

Severe Rule

Besides peace, however, the Taliban also brought the strictest interpretation of the **sharia**, Islamic law, anywhere in the world. The Taliban punished thieves by cutting off their hands or feet. They forced all Afghan men to grow beards and to abandon Western clothing. Girls were not allowed to go to school. Women were forbidden to work outside their homes. Whenever they left their home, women had to wear a **burqa**.

The only open area in a burqa is a mesh strip at eye level, 3 inches (7.6 centimeters) square, that allows the woman to see. Women were supposed to do all the household chores and were forbidden to talk or laugh in public or travel on a bus without a

In July 2000, Pakistani soccer players were forced to shave their heads as a punishment for violating the Taliban dress code by wearing shorts when Taliban forces raided their playing field in Kandahar in southern Afghanistan.

man present or a written note giving permission to ride.

The Taliban banned many activities that were considered "un-Islamic." These included watching television, going to the movies, using a computer, flying kites, and playing board games. Dancing, listening to music, and playing a musical instrument were forbidden. Afghans were not allowed to hang paintings, photographs, or other art on the walls of their homes or offices, because a strict interpretation of sharia bans visual representations of people. All windows had to be painted black so that no one would be able to see inside.

The Taliban's religious police force ensured that everyone obeyed the new rules. Often the police punished wrongdoers on the spot. There are stories of women being beaten because they had an inch of ankle showing below their burqa or they made too much noise as they walked.

The world's tallest standing Buddha statue was destroyed by the Taliban in March 2001, along with all other statues, which were deemed insulting to Islam.

The severe nature of Taliban rule was criticized even by Iran, which itself has a strict Islamic society. Iran's leader, Ayatollah Ali Khamenei, said that what the Taliban were doing was "neither connected to Islam nor accepted by it... [the Taliban] are... far from human realities."

In March 2001, the Taliban ordered the destruction of two giant Buddhist statues at Bamiyan, Afghanistan. The statues had been carved into the side of a cliff by artists during the Kushan empire, seventeen hundred years ago. One statue stood 125 feet (38 meters) high and the other 175 feet (53 m) high. The United Nations Educational, Scientific and Cultural Organization (UNESCO) and many world governments pleaded with the Taliban to preserve the statues as part of the world's cultural heritage. To the Taliban, however, the statues were forbidden by Islam because they encouraged "idol worship." The Taliban blew the statues up with dynamite.

Al-Qaeda Attack

One of the strongest supporters of the Taliban was Osama bin Laden. In 1996 he returned from Saudi Arabia to Afghanistan, where he hoped to set up al-Qaeda training camps. In 1997, he moved to Kandahar, where he and Mullah Omar became friends. The Taliban leader promised to provide protection for bin Laden and al-Qaeda. Mullah Omar gave several training camps to al-Qaeda. Now, from his base in Afghanistan, bin Laden urged his followers to strike against the United States.

In 1998, al-Qaeda bombed U.S. embassies in Kenya and Tanzania. More than 250 people were killed and five thousand were injured. On September 11, 2001, al-Qaeda terrorists hijacked four airplanes in the United States. Two planes rammed the twin towers of New York's World Trade Center and one crashed into the Pentagon. The fourth plane crashed into a Pennsylvania field before it could reach its target. The passengers, who had heard about the other attacks on their cell phones, overpowered their highjackers. More than three thousand people died in these attacks. A shocked and angry United States blamed Afghanistan and its protection of bin Laden, the man behind the attacks.

The south tower of the World Trade Center in New York City begins its collapse as smoke billows from both towers on September 11, 2001. The 110-story towers were brought down by two hijacked airplanes that were used as weapons by al-Qaeda operatives intent on destroying a symbol of prosperity in the United States. Two other planes were also hijacked and crashed. About 3,000 people died in these attacks.

CHAPTER 5

The Fall of the Taliban

Almost immediately after the September 11, 2001, attacks, the United States demanded that the Taliban surrender Osama bin Laden and other al-Qaeda leaders. Mullah Omar, however, said that bin Laden was a "guest" of the Taliban and refused to turn him over.

The United States decided to act. It assembled a large military force in the Middle East, the Persian Gulf, and the Indian Ocean. The aircraft carrier

Modern and ancient forms of warfare were combined in the U.S.-led coalition attack on Taliban and al-Qaeda forces in Afghanistan in November 2001. Master Sgt. Bart Decker, Air Force Special Tactics Operator, is pictured on horseback in a wooden saddle as he accompanies hundreds of Afghan Northern Alliance horsemen fighting in the Balkh Valley on their way to the Mazar-e Sharif region.

Carl Vinson, along with supporting ships and planes, was already in the Persian Gulf. Another aircraft carrier, the *Enterprise*, was in the Arabian Sea. On September 19, a third carrier, the *Theodore Roosevelt*, sailed with a number of other ships toward the Persian Gulf from Norfolk, Virginia. At the same time, a fourth carrier, the *Kitty Hawk*, left its base in Japan, packed with battle helicopters. The United States also prepared special operations and quick response troops for action in Afghanistan.

Pakistan's President Musharraf, who had supported the Taliban, switched sides to ally Pakistan with the United States. Mullah Omar once again refused to turn bin Laden over to the United States.

The United States presented its evidence that al-Qaeda was behind the September 11 attacks to NATO. NATO approved U.S. action in Afghanistan.

War Begins

On October 6, 2001, President Bush issued a final warning to the Taliban to turn over bin Laden and the other leaders of al-Qaeda. Again, the Taliban refused. The next day, the war in Afghanistan, named "Operation Enduring Freedom," began when U.S. and British planes hit targets inside Afghanistan.

Some forty land-based and carrier-based bombers struck Taliban targets. British and American ships in the Arabian Sea also launched cruise missiles at targets inside Afghanistan. Cruise missiles can be programmed to fly low over the landscape and hit a precise target from hundreds of miles away. The next day, B-52 and B-1B high-altitude heavy bombers from the Indian Ocean base of Diego Garcia dropped their bombs on Taliban bases.

The opening air attack was designed to destroy the terrorist training camps run by al-Qaeda and the Taliban. American and British special operations soldiers also landed on the ground in Afghanistan. They joined up with the Northern Alliance, a collection of Afghan groups that had been resisting the Taliban since 1994. The Northern Alliance's base was in the northeastern

In the frontline village of Rabat, near Bagram, 30 miles (48 km) from Kabul, Northern Alliance fighters march toward their position before attacking Taliban-controlled positions north of the capital in mid-November 2001.

part of Afghanistan, which had never been under Taliban rule.

The bombing continued throughout October, forcing the Taliban out of cities and into the countryside. There, bombing strikes were directed at Taliban forces by U.S. special operations forces on the ground.

Fall of Kabul

In late October, the United States beefed up its air strikes in support of Northern Alliance forces attacking the Taliban. The air strikes helped the Northern Alliance, now with more powerful weapons, provided by the United States and Great Britain, to push Taliban forces back toward Kabul. The war continued to intensify into November. Abdul Rashid Dostum, a Northern Alliance general, joined other anti-Taliban fighters to attack the Taliban-held city of Mazar-e Sharif. The attackers quickly captured the local airport and moved toward the city's center. Taliban fighters, seeing that the city was lost, switched sides and joined the attackers. Mazar-e Sharif fell on November 11, followed by the fall of the city of Herat on November 12. On November 13, Kabul itself fell to the Northern Alliance.

In mid-November, the Fifteenth U.S. Marine Expeditionary Unit, a force of twenty-five hundred marines, landed south of Kandahar. Except for small special operations forces, the Fifteenth was the first unit of U.S. ground troops in the war. The marines helped anti-Taliban forces capture Kandahar on December 7.

Escape from Tora Bora

The last Afghan province held by the Taliban surrendered on December 9—two months after the war had begun. Only days before, Hamid Karzai had been chosen to be the head of an interim Afghan government.

The enemy, however, was not completely defeated. Both Mullah Omar and Osama bin Laden had yet to be captured. The United States knew that bin Laden had fled from Jalalabad to Tora Bora, about 30 miles (48 km) to the south. There, al-Qaeda had built a series of trenches and fortified caves in the foothills of the mountains.

While U.S. planes pounded the area with bombing runs, American forces enlisted two Afghan warlords to help them capture the al-Qaeda leader. The warlords estimated that bin Laden had about fifteen hundred of his best fighters with him at Tora Bora. Instead of using U.S. forces, the United States decided to let the warlords go in to root out bin Laden. Unfortunately, the two warlords were rivals and did not work well together. Somehow, between November 28 and November 30, 2001, bin Laden was actually able to walk out

A coalition force of U.S., Canadian, and Afghan infantry units waits to be picked up by helicopter in the Tora Bora region of Afghanistan in May 2002. The troops were in the region on an intelligence-gathering operation.

of Tora Bora into thick pine forests and—as far as experts know—escape to Pakistan. By not using its own soldiers, the United States had lost a "golden opportunity" to capture the al-Qaeda leader, said a U.S. intelligence officer. Later, Tora Bora would fall, but most of the al-Qaeda fighters, like bin Laden, had already escaped. Although it failed to capture bin Laden and Mullah Omar, the United States did capture hundreds of prisoners in the Afghan war. More than six hundred of them were eventually jailed at the U.S. naval base at Guantanamo Bay, Cuba.

A force of twenty thousand U.S. and NATO troops remains in Afghanistan to continue fighting the remnants of the Taliban and al-Qaeda, mainly in eastern and southern Afghanistan.

Progress and Its Threats

Today, Afghanistan has made much progress in building a new democracy. Women are now free to vote, work, drive, and even appear in public without a male relative by their side. The new parliament elected in October 2005 has enacted laws to help the country rebuild and strengthen its new freedoms. A free press now operates in Afghanistan's major cities.

A woman wearing a burqa votes in Afghanistan's presidential election on October 9, 2004. Afghans were voting for a new president for the first time in twenty years.

The United States and European nations, joined by Pakistan and Iran, have spent billions of dollars to help Afghanistan rebuild after more than twenty years of war. Five million Afghan children were in school at the beginning of 2006, up from 900,000 at the beginning of 2001. Roads, hospitals, and power plants are being rebuilt. More than 3.5 million Afghan refugees have returned to Afghanistan from Pakistan and Iran. Some 800,000 Afghan refugees, however, are still living in Iran and three million in Pakistan. Both Iran and Pakistan want

FAST FACT

Political cartoons often use humor in order to make people think about an issue. Cartoons are not designed to provoke widespread rioting. Yet that is what happened when news spread throughout the Muslim world in early February 2006 that a Danish newspaper had published cartoons depicting the Prophet Muhammad, the founder of Islam. In Islam, showing an image of Muhammad is blasphemy, an insult to God. Muslims viewed this act as a direct attack by the Danes and other Europeans on the Muslim religion. On February 4, Muslims in Syria attacked the Danish embassy in Damascus. On February 5, angry demonstrators burned the Danish embassy in Beirut. The next day, protests erupted all over Afghanistan. Five protesters were killed by police. Three more protesters were killed on February 7. "This is something that really upset Afghans," said Joanna Nathan, a European analyst.

The Case of Abdul Rahman

Just how different the country of Afghanistan is from a Western democracy became very apparent in March 2006. The difference revolved around the rights of an Afghan man who wanted to choose his own religion.

Abdul Rahman had moved to Pakistan in the mid-1990s. There he converted from Islam to Christianity. After living in Europe for a while, he returned to Afghanistan. In March 2006, he was arrested and brought to trial before a judge. His crime under Afghanistan's Islamic law code: abandoning Islam and converting to Christianity. The penalty for such a crime is death.

The idea that someone could be executed for choosing another religion shocked and outraged much of the non-Muslim world. World religious leaders and heads of state, including President George W. Bush and Pope Benedict XVI, urged the Afghan government to release Rahman. The requests put Afghan president Hamid Karzai in a very difficult position: If he let Rahman go free, it would look as if the United States and Europe were telling him what to do. That would make the Afghan government very unstable, because polls showed that the overwhelming majority of Afghans supported death for Rahman.

On March 28, the crisis seemed to end calmly, when the case was dismissed, and Abdul Rahman was quietly released from prison. His whereabouts are unknown, but there are reports he was granted asylum in another country.

the refugees to leave because of the high cost of maintaining refugee camps and rising tensions between refugees and local governments.

Early in 2006, the Afghan government and seventy donor nations held a major meeting in London, England, to discuss what further aid Afghanistan needs from the international community. At the end of the meeting, the world leaders signed a five-year development plan called the Afghanistan Compact. The United States promised $1.1 billion in aid and Great Britain promised $800 million.

Yet despite much progress, the forces that seek to overthrow the Karzai government have become more active.

"This is a transitional time for Afghanistan," Raz Mahamat, an official who deals with returned refugees, has said. "We are struggling between hope and hopelessness. That is the reality."

Time Line

6000 B.C.	Afghans practice herding and farming.
3000 B.C.	Afghans live in villages.
1500 B.C.	Indo-Europeans enter Afghanistan.
540 B.C.	Persians conquer Bactria.
329 B.C.	Alexander the Great conquers Afghanistan.
304 B.C.	The Mauryas conquer southern Afghanistan; Buddhism is introduced.
A.D. 50	Kushans conquer Afghanistan.
652	Arabs invade Afghanistan; Islam is introduced.
998–1030	Reign of Mahmud of Ghazna.
1221	Mongols under Genghis Khan invade Afghanistan.
1504–1530	Reign of Babur.
1747	Ahmad Khan Abdali founds a dynasty that reigns until 1973.
1839–1842	First Anglo-Afghan War.
1878–1880	Second Anglo-Afghan War.
1973	Muhammad Daoud seizes power and establishes a republic.
1979–1989	Soviet Union invades and occupies Afghanistan.
1980	Osama bin Laden goes to Afghanistan to fight the Soviets.
1988	Al-Qaeda founded in Afghanistan.
1994	The Taliban gain control of Afghanistan.
2001	September 11: Al-Qaeda terrorists hijack U.S. airliners and attack the United States, killing thousands; October 7: U.S. and British planes begin bombing Afghanistan.
2002	Transitional government is formed for Afghanistan.
2003	NATO takes command of international military forces in Afghanistan.
2004	January 4: Afghan constitution is adopted; October 9: Hamid Karzai is elected president of Afghanistan.
2005	October 6: Afghan parliamentary elections are held.
2006	January 31–February 1: International conference on aid to Afghanistan meets in London, England; March 28: Christian released after facing death penalty for abandoning Islam and converting to Christianity.

Glossary

Achaemenid Empire Persian empire founded by Cyrus the Great in 538 B.C.

al-Qaeda an Islamic terrorist organization started in 1988 by Osama bin Laden

atheism the belief that there is no divine power

Buddhism a religion that teaches that conduct, wisdom, and meditation release one from suffering

burqa long, pleated woman's garment that covers the body from head to toe

constitution the basic principles and laws of a nation

Cyrus the Great king of Persia and founder of the Persian empire (600–529 B.C.)

dictatorship a government ruled by one person who has absolute power

ethnic describing a group with a common culture

Hindu term applied to the religion and culture of the majority of people in India

infidels people who do not believe in a particular religion

insurgents people who rebel against the established government

Islam world religion founded by Muhammad (570–632)

jihad Islamic holy war

madrasas Islamic schools

mosques Muslim houses of worship

mujahideen Islamic guerrilla fighters

mullah Islamic religious leader

National Liberation Front (NLF) a political party in Afghanistan and a term often used by anti-government groups who want to liberate their country from an oppressive government

NATO an alliance of the United States, Canada, and a number of European nations to promote world security

parliament the national legislature of a country

Pashtuns main ethnic group in Afghanistan

Persian Gulf body of water between Saudi Arabia and Iran

Pukhtunwali the Pashtun code of behavior

revolutionaries armed civilians who support the struggle for revolution and reform of a government or society

sharia the religious law of Islam, embracing all aspects of a Muslim's life

Tajiks Afghan ethnic group related to Iranians

Taliban radical group that ruled Afghanistan from 1994 to 2001

warlords local commanders with private armies

For More Information

Books

Akbar, Said Hyder. *Come Back to Afghanistan: A California Teenager's Story.* Bloomsbury, 2005.

Banting, Erinn. *Afghanistan: The Culture.* Crabtree, 2003.

Banting, Erinn. *Afghanistan: The Land.* Crabtree, 2003.

Banting, Erinn. *Afghanistan: The People.* Crabtree, 2003.

Ewans, Martin. *Afghanistan: A Short History.* Harper Collins, 2002.

Latifa. *My Forbidden Face: Growing Up Under the Taliban.* Hyperion, 2001.

Web Sites

www.afghanistans.com/
   Afghanistan's official Web site

www.afghan-network.net/Culture/
   Culture and history of Afghanistan

www.nationalgeographic.com/landincrisis/education.html
   Geographic site with links to many Afghan sites

www.state.gov/r/pa/ei/bgn/5380.htm
   The most up-to-date information about Afghanistan from the U.S. Department of State Fact Book

Publisher's note to educators and parents: Our editors have carefully reviewed these Web sites to ensure that they are suitable for children. Many Web sites change frequently, however, and we cannot guarantee that a site's future contents will continue to meet our high standards of quality and educational value. Be advised that children should be closely supervised whenever they access the Internet.

Index

About the Author

Charles Piddock is a former editor in chief of Weekly Reader Corporation, publisher of sixteen classroom magazines for schools from pre-K through high school, including *Current Events, Current Science,* and *Teen Newsweek.* In his career with Weekly Reader, he has written and edited hundreds of articles for young people of all ages on world and national affairs, science, literature, and other topics. Before working at Weekly Reader, he worked in publishing in New York City and, before that, served as a Peace Corps volunteer in rural West Bengal, India.